CHAMPIONS
NEVER MAKE
COLD CALLS

the publishing CIRCLE

For permission requests, write to the publisher, addressed "Attention: Permissions Coordinator," at the address below.

admin@ThePublishingCircle.com
or
THE PUBLISHING CIRCLE
Regarding: Danny Creed
19215 SE 34th Street
Suite 106-347
Camas, Washington 98607

DISCLAIMER: The Publisher and the Author make no representations or warranties with respect to the accuracy or completeness of the contents of this work and specifically disclaim all warranties, including without limitation, warranties of fitness for a particular purpose. No warranty may be created or extended by sales or promotional materials. The advice and strategies contained herein may not be suitable for every situation. This work is sold with the understanding that the Publisher is not engaged in rendering legal, accounting, or other professional services. If professional assistance is required, the services of a competent professional person should be sought. Neither the Publisher, nor the Author shall be liable for damages arising herefrom.

The fact that an organization or website is referred to in this work as a citation and/or a potential source of further information does not mean that the Author or Publisher endorses the information the organization or website may provide or recommendations it may make. Further, readers should be aware that internet websites listed in this work may have changed or disappeared between when this work was written and when it is read. The Publisher is not responsible for the author's website, other mentioned websites, expired weblinks, or content of any website that is not owned by the publisher.

All content is the author's opinion only.

CHAMPIONS' NETWORK and its conversation bubble are trademarks of Danny Creed.

CHAMPIONS NEVER MAKE COLD CALLS / DANNY CREED
ISBN 978-1-947398-68-9 paperback
ISBN 978-1-947398-69-6 large-print paperback
ISBN 978-1-947398-70-2 hardback
ISBN 978-1-947398-73-3 ebook

Book design by Michele Uplinger

For full information on booking Dan Creed
for personal or professional business coaching,
or to speak at your next meeting,
please visit www.realworldbusinesscoach.com
or call us directly at (602) 697-5949

• • •

This book is dedicated to the greatest salesman I've ever had the privilege of knowing and learning from. Many years ago, Dale McCoy believed in a Kansas farm boy and took the risk of allowing him to sell airtime at a local radio station. For over 40 years now, I continue to utilize the techniques and lessons that he introduced me to.

Dale's son, Marc McCoy is also a great businessman; sales pro; creative guru; author and dear friend. Selling is the foundation for everything. Everyone is a salesperson, whether they know it or not. I am deeply proud to be a sales professional. Without these men and friends, my life would be considerably different.

Thanks, Dale, you are remembered.

Thanks, Marc, you are a true friend.

• • •

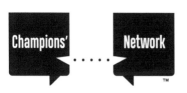

CHAMPIONS NEVER MAKE COLD CALLS

*High-Impact
Low-Cost
Lead Generation*

DANNY CREED

CONTENTS · · ·

The Fail-Proof System

Champions'

"*All businesses are about three things: skills, doors, and **Champions.** The doors open and they will open on occasion for any business coach. A **Champion** will help open those doors for you, or they're on the other side of the door and they open it and let you in. But a **Champion** is not interested in anyone without formidable skills. So, a Business Coach can only really effectively advance their interests by getting skillful, and then they get recognized hopefully by a **Champion** who will help them open doors.*"

Network

PARAPHRASED FROM A QUOTE BY PAT FRALEY,
ADAPTED BY BUSINESS COACH DAN CREED

WELCOME TO THE CHAMPIONS' POWER REFERRAL Network. I devised the process and strategy behind this system through years of trial and error and frustration. Like anyone who has ever sold anything, we know that prospects and customers just do not fall from a tree. They come from lots of hard work and sometimes (particularly in the past) lots of cold calling. Great prospects and new customers also are a product of smart marketing and calculated networking and several other time-intensive activities.

At first, I thought it would be insane to think I could achieve all of these strategies. If I did, how would I have time to sell to the leads that I generated? The problem was obvious, but I didn't know what to do about it. Most of the experts in the field at that time didn't know what to do either. Everyone who taught successful selling seemed to avoid that issue. I read all the books about selling and prospecting, but none pointed me to a simple way to get everything done using one strategy. It made sense to me that a simple strategy to accomplish all the "required" activities was what was needed.

Another thing that made a lot of sense was that the pressure of finding prospects should never be solely on my shoulders. I observed many salespeople struggling, working long hours trying to find qualified prospects. Their success was based on how many of their limited hours they spent in front of prospects.

That is a huge weight for anyone to bear.

A solution came to mind. I decided to focus on how I might build a massive army of "referral" agents—people who either knew me and liked me, respected me, loved me, or simply wanted to help me. People who would readily refer me to others when and if they had a chance.

The challenge to set up a system where this would work not only for me, but for others, was on. This led to years of piecing together the thoughts of some of the top minds in the sales business and adding those to my own experiences. The result of my focus was the development of the Champions' Power Referral Network for lead generation, a system that has proven to be overwhelmingly successful.

I use this system every day. Because I do, I've built a successful, world-class business-coaching practice. It's allowed me to profitably build large sales organizations and I've used it in thirteen entrepreneurial startups. I have taught this system to my local and international sales staff for years. I have trained thousands of professional salespeople to use this system. It was created through a burning desire to change and adjust to the market. Simply put . . .

IT WORKS!
BUT THERE ARE
NO SHORTCUTS!

The concepts of the program are not new. You will have heard about some of the concepts, although some will be fresh. But what the Champions' Power Referral Network does is put the most powerful—and sometimes simple techniques—into one cohesive blueprint. The system encompasses all the secrets of prospecting, networking, marketing, priority/time management skills, and sales strategies that promise to propel those who use them to the top of their field.

RESULTS:

- Since 2007, I have NEVER made a cold call. I know

how to do those and I'm good at doing them, but I would rather go to a prospect because I've been recommended by one of their trusted colleagues.

- I average over 150 face-to-face prospect meetings a year, all coming from my Champions' Power Referral Network.

- For more than a decade, every new client I acquire comes from a referral from someone in my Champions' Power Referral Network

- I've stopped going to big, worthless networking meetings where 90% of attendees were not my prospects. I only attend small, focused meetings where 90% of the attendees ARE my prospects. Using my formula, there's little time wasted attending worthless events which gives me more time with my clients and my family.

Champions' Power Referral Network factoid: No matter your profession, to be *successful* you must be a salesperson. And, a successful salesperson is fundamentally a leads-generation expert.

Simply put, show me a struggling business professional and I'll show you a "frustrated and struggling" salesperson. In turn, I'll show you a salesperson who doesn't know how to generate leads or, in many cases, is someone who doesn't want to put the work in that is required to generate leads.

This system proves to work with experienced sales professionals. It also proves to be just as effective for a new salesperson. In addition, it is a simple and phenomenally successful tool for executives who are now, possibly for the first time in their career, required to sell. That's because the Champions' Power Referral Network has proven to be a powerful lead generation system that is ongoing and systematic.

One of the best salespeople I've ever known used to say "Filling the sales funnel was not the hard part. The hard part is keeping the funnel full!" Basically, it's fairly easy to generate a few leads and put them in the sales funnel or pipeline. But cut off the flow of leads and you'll find yourself with *no leads, no prospects, no customers, and no job.*

There are two major benefits of the Champions' Power Referral Network for lead generation. The first is eliminating cold calling.

NEVER, EVER DO ANOTHER COLD CALL!

A major benefit of my system eliminates the age-old bugaboo of every salesperson that has ever existed (whether they admit it or not) and that's generating the energy and the nerve to do cold calls! No one likes cold calling.

And just to be clear, my distaste for the practice starts with the premise that cold calling is the poorest use of a salesperson's time I can imagine. It's random. It's unfocused. It's intrusive . . .and in today's marketplace, intrusive is not welcome.

Your odds are better if you took a week and your life savings and went to Vegas. Think about it. You're randomly contacting hundreds of people who don't know you, don't trust you, and initially don't care who you are or what you want . . .and you're trying to get them to sit down with you so you can tell them why they should talk with you some more.

Cold calling has no doubt been the foundation of many

sales organizations of the past and the technique once worked. Today, it is a technique of the past and it isn't an acceptable strategy for the successful salesperson in the challenging market we now face. Why? The market has changed. Technology triggered this change. The constant and rapid advancement of technology has changed consumers (our customers and prospects) and we had better understand just what that means if we want to be successful.

Here's how that's reflected: any information that a customer or prospect wants, they can now get in a matter of seconds through their computer, notepad, or handheld communication device. In fact, some research now suggests that as much as seventy percent of all buying decisions are now made *prior to a first meeting.* So, the whole idea of cold calling has been turned upside down. Basically, this means that when a consumer needs a product or service, they now go straight to their communication device of choice. They Google for the information or resource they need and get an instantaneous list. From this list, they then interview suppliers of the product or service. So, while a salesperson may go into a first meeting and treat it as a "discovery" meeting, the fact is, the prospect sees the meeting as a second meeting because they've already done their research. They will expect you to have done your research as well, dispensing with the traditional questions such as, "So, can you tell me a little about your business?" The prospect of today expects you to have already done that research, just as they have researched you and your competitors.

The change in buying patterns is obvious. Consumers/customers/prospects do not want or need to be cold called. There was a time that worked, but that time is over and the sooner you understand this and apply more accepted techniques, the sooner you will become an effective salesperson in this digital age.

As salespeople, we must look for ways to find prospects who already know what they want and need. We had better be interacting with prospects and clients and sell to them in a way they want to be sold to, not the way we've always done it.

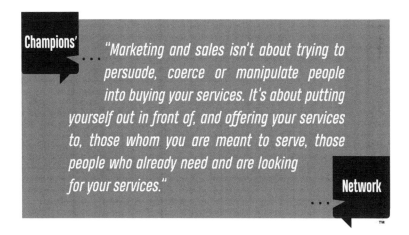

Champions' ... *"Marketing and sales isn't about trying to persuade, coerce or manipulate people into buying your services. It's about putting yourself out in front of, and offering your services to, those whom you are meant to serve, those people who already need and are looking for your services."* **Network** ...

MICHAEL PORT

What the prospect wants today is understanding. UNDERSTANDING! This is the ability to *ask not tell*. This is the ability to work together in a complimentary, "no-pitch" environment where both parties are simply evaluating to see if there are obvious needs one of them have that can be solved by the other person. Then, and only then, can an exchange happen. We must start this process through the "referral" from a trusted friend or advisor to your future prospect. This eliminates the age-old fear-of-being-sold emotion where a prospect is on guard immediately when a conversation begins. Through this referral process, we enter customer relationships with the sole purpose of having a great conversation that's focused around understanding the prospect's needs from their point of view and then, and only then, determine if it is logical to work together. Once that happens, you can embark on an agreement.

Let's recap the ground we've covered so far.

- Telemarketing and cold calling strategies are disruptive and intrusive.

- Prospects and consumers have unlimited access to information and research on every person and every business.

- Most prospecting strategies are highly time-consuming.

Successful sales are a matter of establishing priorities and managing the time around achieving the highest-priority and highest-consequence tasks—and cold calling in today's market is neither efficient nor a high priority.

Here's how we change our selling paradigm. In the same amount of time you previously used to make random calls, you can now, with focused networking and targeted conversations, talk with ten, twenty, thirty, or more prospects who know they need help because they've already done the research. They also know and understand the value of your product and service and are ready to select someone who offers what they need. They are ready to buy.

Once I implemented my Champions' Power Referral Network process, prospects immediately wanted to talk to me because the meeting was established on their terms. Most knew they had a need and needed some help. They were solid candidates ready to hire me and use my services.

After all, how can you possibly claim genuine interest and concern about a prospect's needs if you have just randomly called them? Selling everything from coaching to selling refrigerators is a personal and emotional issue, and that's true for whatever product or service you represent.

The bottom line is that my prospecting process drastically improves from a random series of events, to referrals from trusted resources for extremely specific opportunities. I improve my time and priority management by 1000% doing more targeted work in less than half of the traditional time spent prospecting.

The second major benefit of the Champions' Power Referral Network is that it allows you to build a huge *personal* sales team of thousands of supporters, for little or no cost.

YOU EASILY SELL YOURSELF!

Most salespeople carry the burden of selling their products and services, selling their talents, selling their product's advantages, and also have all the marketing efforts completely on their shoulders. Successful entrepreneurs the world over will tell you the hardest way to build a business is to try to do it all by yourself.

The Champions' Power Referral Network system builds a huge network of referral "agents" who are constantly recommending you and referring you because they know you, like you, believe in you, and honestly want to help you. I would much rather have 2,000 people thinking about me and recommending me than try to reach that many people all by myself. With this system, you now have that power and it should not cost you more than the price of a cheeseburger.

NOTHING IS EASY

Change is everywhere! Change is necessary! Change and flexibility are required mindsets today for any level of success. Change is happening faster today than ever before and will continue to do so. We cannot stop it. So, absolute acceptance of our current atmosphere is required. If you don't like the way things are . . .tough! There is nothing you can do to stop it, and without change, you will be left behind.

In my *Straight Talk—Thriving In Business* workshop I discuss the 7 LAWS OF BUSINESS SURVIVAL. The first law is:

**"If you continue to do business
the way you've always done business
then YOU WILL be out of business!"**

It is essential that we understand our prospects and customers and *earn* their business. The key is to get them to open up and talk to us. *The best way to accomplish that is for your call or appointment to be the result of a suggestion or recommendation from someone that your new prospect knows and trusts.* That is exactly how the Champions' Power Referral Network works.

In Malcom Gladwell's bestselling book, *The Tipping Point*, he defines these people as "connectors" or "the people in a community who know large numbers of people and who are in the habit of making introductions."

Implementing a successful system to find these people is not always easy. It requires discipline. This is the kind of discipline that requires day in, day out, dedication. This is the kind of discipline most salespeople do not take the time to learn and practice.

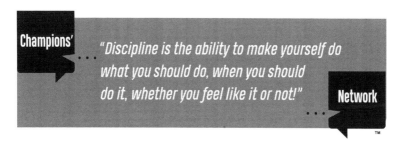

Champions' ... *"Discipline is the ability to make yourself do what you should do, when you should do it, whether you feel like it or not!"* Network
...

ELBERT HUBBARD

Top salespeople understand this definition of discipline, are good at applying discipline, and have mastered it. Why? Because *the end result of focused discipline is always success.* No matter what, they always do what they know they need to do and when they need to do it. That doesn't mean they always like to do it or even want to do it, but (and here's the kicker), they do it.

You must learn to challenge everything you once knew or thought you knew about selling. This especially applies to how we think about our customers. One of the greatest changes of the last decade is the way consumers now make their buying decisions. These changes are a direct reflection on how the consumer/prospect/customer have themselves changed. As I've already shared, that's due to technology. People are also now making buying decisions, more than ever before, based on "old-school" emotional reasons. These two shifts have changed how we find prospects and how we position ourselves to be found.

Most traditional media doesn't work anymore. Neither do many of the "fad" social-media platforms. Today, we need to protect our time and not get caught up in the "I'll try it for a while and see if it works" syndrome. We must be absolutely clear about who our perfect client is; how you can help them, based on their needs; where they get their information; and who they know.

KEEPING THE FUNNEL FULL

I have continuously used the Champions' Power Referral Network system for over thirty-five years in one form or another. Through its use, I have become highly successful and feel blessed to have built my entrepreneurial and business coaching career this way. My success has largely been due to the fact that this system has continuously provided qualified prospects for me to meet with—and eventually they ask to buy my services. Because this happens, it allows me to use my time efficiently and effectively, which translates into monetary value.

There is an old adage in the sales game that you must "fill the sales funnel." In this case, the "funnel" is an imaginary receptacle where all your leads and prospects go. In sales, it is always essential that you have a number of prospects that you are working with at the same time. This business truly is a game of numbers, one that creates an equation as to how many prospects you need to get a certain amount of sales. Your sales funnel is the key, but I learned a long time ago that filling the funnel with prospects was not the hard part. The hard part was *keeping the funnel full.* Many salespeople will work hard for a while to fill their funnel, then stop working on their funnel. A month or two will pass and they then find themselves needing more customers, and more sales . . . but their funnel is empty. At this point, there is nothing left to do but take the time-consuming route of starting all over again to refill their sales-prospect funnel. The key is having a system to consistently generate leads that fill your funnel and keep it full. This is what the Champions' Power Referral Network does.

I understood from the beginning that you *must* sell a customer *before* you can coach them. I also realized that the more clients I sold into my programs, the less time I would have to prospect for new clients. For that reason, the successful implementation of the Champions' Power Referral Network was paramount. And as I believed it would, it worked in a spectacular fashion. Since 2008 I have consistently generated over 150 prospect presentations annually. That's almost four meetings per week, every week! The only way I could generate this many leads was to:

1. Consistently keep my sales-prospect funnel full.

2. Have a powerful and effective system that generates the leads to keep the funnel full.

3. Have a system that consistently creates quality "perfect customer" leads to fill the funnel.

Every year, this system has consistently produced hot leads for me and, more importantly, produced customers at a low cost-per-customer acquisition rate. Note that I did not say cost-per-lead; I said cost-per-customer! Using this system can often eliminate the need for the many forms of expensive marketing we've been told we need. It's just not necessary if you use the Champions' Power Referral Network correctly. In fact, my number one marketing expense in the last decade has been taking my Champions to lunch.

The Champions' Power Referral Network is easily reflected in a similar model that LinkedIn developed that is highly successful. Their model follows this format:

connections>leads>appointments>proposals>sales>new sales funnel

The significant difference between LinkedIn's system and the Champions' Power Referral Network is that users of the Champions' Network don't have to work hard to gain fruitful connections.

Since about 1980, I have never made a cold call. With this system, you simply do not have to make cold calls anymore. Telemarketing is involved, but it's a different style of telemarketing. It is one that focuses on a *non-abrasive, non-threatening, non-intrusive* form of telemarketing that simply works. It works because the traditional "tell 'em and sell 'em" approach is turned upside down by transforming a "pitch" into an enjoyable conversation. That's what prospects and customers want. They want someone who is interested in what they need and want. They want to talk to someone who they think actually cares about their wants and needs. So, give them what they want and sell more in less time.

There are many referral gimmicks and systems and resources available. The Champions' Power Referral Network was developed with a desire to improve time efficiency in the process of finding new clients. Many sales systems and salespeople I knew were cold-calling, networking, going to marketing meetings, and more. That meant they had to do at least three somewhat disparate activities every week. No one wants to do that. This is one of the reasons any salesperson wants to at least give the Champions' Power Referral Network a try.

The system is not rocket science, however, to quote an old and wise street mentor that I was blessed to know in the early 1980s . . .

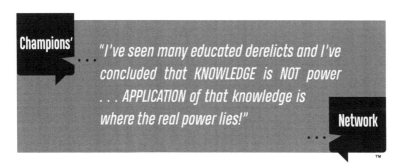

"I've seen many educated derelicts and I've concluded that KNOWLEDGE is NOT power . . . APPLICATION of that knowledge is where the real power lies!"

ALBERT EINSTEIN

To make the Champions' Power Referral Network work, you must implement it completely.

Do not skip a single step.

Do NOT just do parts of the system, do it all. Some of it may seem trivial—that's where the secrets are found. There are certain elements of this system that you may be familiar with, but don't let that keep you from implementing this system completely. It's the nuances and slight changes that represent the power of the system. Again, it is a mix of networking strategies and referral strategies rolled into one single system rather than two or three or four specific strategies. It is one system that works and meshes together to form a cohesive no-fail strategy.

Stop and simply take a moment to decide

**"Am I willing to make the commitment to doing this?
If I do, will I be disciplined and exact in its implementation?"**

If your answer is yes on both counts, then it's now time to move forward!

This is going to be fun and profitable. Let's get started!

CHAPTER 1

The Champions' Power Referral Network

Building your
CHAMPIONS, SUPER CHAMPIONS and ELITE CHAMPIONS

T HE CHAMPIONS' POWER REFERRAL NETWORK is a powerful, effective, and proven process that is based on the foundational elements of relationship building and communication. I will say this again later, but always remember that one of the greatest forms of financial leverage is through the contacts you have already created and those you will create in the future. *Knowing* the right people, *knowing* the right people who know the people you need to know, and *being known* by them, can open doors that can save you years of hard work. The quality and quantity of your contacts and your relationships will have more to do with your success than perhaps any other factor.

The initial rule is that you must condition yourself to *always* be looking for strategic networking and referral opportunities. ALWAYS! Always look for and meet people who are well connected to people you, in turn, need to connect with. Instead of the usual inefficient approaches to prospecting, networking, marketing, and telemarketing, I focus my efforts on this one question:

"WHO DO I KNOW, WHO KNOWS THE PEOPLE I WANT TO DO BUSINESS WITH?"

The answer to the question usually lies within the people and firms where:

A. I am already a credible resource simply because we have met, which means they are people who

B. already know me, or think they know me, and like me because there is no reason for them not to like me! (People refer people simply because they have met you, no matter how casually) and,

C. people and firms that I know that share my target audience and prospects.

A REMINDER: This may be the most powerful system ever devised for finding prospects and customers. BUT you must use it *exactly* as is explained here. *Exactly!* If you take any shortcuts, it more than likely will not work. If you do take shortcuts and try to second-guess the system, don't come whining to me that the system didn't work for you! It works, it works dramatically well, but you must apply it exactly as I offer it here.

The key to the system is in understanding all of the efficiencies that it creates. While most people treat *marketing, networking,* and *referrals* as three separate functions, the Champions' Power Referral Network treats them as one single hybrid event. If applied exactly, you may be able to vastly exceed your personal and business goals and spend few, if any, marketing dollars.

In some industries, like professional coaching, for instance, it is not only acceptable, but people encourage salespeople to spend upwards of $2,000 for every warm lead that is generated. It's usually suggested that this is accomplished through everything from direct mail, to telemarketing, to networking group fees, and more. Yes, all of these strategies work or have worked. However, all of them can also cost you a lot of your precious marketing budget if they don't work. Heck, some of these require you to pay a year in advance, with no recourse if they don't work.

Using the Champions' Power Referral Network my current *cost per customer acquisition* is under $10.00. That's correct, less than $10.00 *per customer.* Currently, my biggest marketing expense is taking my tier-two Super Champions and tier-three Elite Champions to lunch.

The Champions' Power Referral Network is made up of three parts.

The concept behind this entire process is that everyone you know, or think you know, has an entire hidden network of people or customers that they know, and you don't know. In other words, *WHO DO YOU KNOW THAT KNOWS THE PEOPLE YOU WANT and NEED TO KNOW?* Throughout this process, we will position ourselves in different ways to earn the right to be referred to these people when and if they ever need our product.

Let's define each level of the Pyramid.

- **Level One: CHAMPIONS' POWER REFERRAL NETWORK:**
The Champions' Power Referral Network is made up of everyone you know or think you know—*everyone*. Experts will tell us that everyone knows at least 200 people. This includes friends, neighbors, waitresses and waiters at your favorite restaurant, family members, etc.

Goal

Our goal is to document every one of these people by name, email, and phone number.

- The purpose of developing and implementing the Champions' Power Referral Network is to achieve "general positioning." At this level, you create an army of people who, at some point in their lives will remember that you are someone they know and like who is in a specific business that they or a friend now need to work with. It might happen at a backyard cookout, or at a dinner party. When your Champion is told by someone at the same event that they are thinking about hiring someone in your area of expertise, they think of you. The result we want is for your Champion to say, "You know, I know someone who does that and they're good at it. Can I recommend them to you?" They continue to recommend you to their acquaintances and their network whenever the occasion arises.

- **Level Two: SUPER CHAMPIONS' POWER REFERRAL NETWORK**: Your Super Champions' Power Referral Network is different than your Level-One Champions' Power Referral Network. Your Super Champion is someone who knows people that you need to know. Your Super Champions' Power Referral Network is focused on the *influencers* you know or would like to know. These are people who are highly influential within their industry or the marketplace. You may have met them briefly at a Chamber of Commerce event, saw them in the newspaper, or you played in a golf league with them. We are going to strategically tap their reservoir of contacts with at least two powerful techniques which, if implemented correctly, will cause your Super Champions to gladly offer specific *personal* referrals for you. Great Super Champions for me have been real estate brokers, insurance professionals, business brokers, financial advisors, Chamber of Commerce leaders, and so on. Again, a perfect Super Champion knows lots of influencers and people that you need to know.

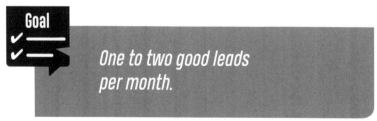

Goal

One to two good leads per month.

- **Level Three: ELITE CHAMPIONS' POWER REFERRAL NETWORK**: The Elite Champions' Power Referral Network group is a completely different level of CHAMPION. The Elite Champion is someone who would make a profitable partner. The process of finding your Elite Champion group is specific and strategic. Elite Champions share one key element with you: Each of you has complimentary customer and contact bases. You're both looking for the same "perfect" client. The only difference is that the budgets you seek come from different pots. This relationship is direct and there is a benefit for each of in offering your respective services to each other's clients and contacts. Great Elite Champions for me are high-end financial advisors, CPAs, and counselors.

Goal

One to two leads a year from each of your Elite Champions' Power Referral Network partners. When you get these leads, you know they will be spectacular leads and that they'll come from people who will usually pay premium rates.

CHAPTER 2

Building your CHAMPIONS' POWER REFERRAL NETWORK System™

1. **PHASE ONE:** Make a list of everyone *you know* or *think you know*. This will eventually be your Champions' Power Referral list to work from. This list may be long. That's okay. My first Champions' Power list was composed of 270 names.

2. The list should include friends, family, friends of the family, people you met at a BBQ in the neighborhood, waitresses or waiters from your favorite restaurants, people that you have a business card from, people you met at a trade show, most of your existing customers (the rest we'll talk about later), and prospects who have said NO. Everyone, and I truly mean everyone, goes on this list. Here's where you put that stack of business cards that's been setting on your desk for months. Every one of

them should be on your Champions' Power list.

3. You'll want to note three things necessary for your initial implementation process:
   a. Name
   b. Email address
   c. Phone number

4. Think about this list as a form of networking. In ordinary networking, everyone usually approaches it strictly as a way to gather cards and give away cards. However, the way I'm asking *you* to think is to change how your mind perceives networking, even if it is as simple as considering all the people that you meet daily. I believe in a simple process that we call The Three Eyes of a Businessperson. The concept is that every salesperson/businessperson, in order to be successful, must possess three specific set of eyes. Or they must have people in place in their business that possess each of these "eyes."

One is the Eye of the entrepreneur. This eye is always looking to the future. Looking forward. Looking for opportunity and options. This eye is eighty percent or more opportunity focused.

The second eye is the Eye of the manager. This eye manages and measures all past results. For instance, this eye keeps track of what you sold yesterday and last week and last month and last year, then compares this to previous years. This eye is key to any business. The third and final eye is the Eye of the Technician. This eye is focused on the here and now. It's focused on the day-to-day tasks of just getting things done. They're always in the present and working on the job. So, when you think about building your Champions' list through networking, you now have switched the eye that you are using. Previously, when networking you entered the networking event with the Eye of the Technician. Now you will put the Eye of the *Entrepreneur* to work for you. This step will allow you to advance in how you do and look at things.

You acquire names differently
Ask for names differently
You ask for appointments differently

The more people that you meet the more opportunity you have to meet the "right" people

5. A key rule: You never know and should never second guess if your friends could be customers. And you should never second guess who your friends and acquaintances might know. Who they know might astound you. This, by the way, is the main "secret" to making this system work. Why? Because everyone always underestimates who their friends, acquaintances, neighbors, and relatives know.

I've taught this system to thousands of business and salespeople, and initially I always ask my students, "Do you know all the people your brother or sister know?" Most people will tell you they don't. The fact is, we all have individual experiences. When it comes to networking effectively, tapping into other people's resources is one of the most underrated and overlooked opportunities available. The goldmine of potential business and sales leads will astound you.

6. **PHASE TWO:** With this list, we take action.

Smile and Dial!

It's time to SMILE and DIAL. CALL ALL OF THEM . . . every darn one of them.

7. Your goal is to have a great conversation while positioning yourself at the same time. There is never any selling whatsoever during these calls. If your Champion even gets a whiff in your conversation that you're trying to sell something, the conversation will be over. Brian Tracy calls this the "LAW OF INDIRECT EFFORT" or the "LAW OF INADVERTENT SELLING." You are selling by not selling. Prospects have two fears—the *fear of being hustled* and the *fear of being taken advantage of!* So do not unleash these fears. This should just be a nice conversation you have with an acquaintance.

8. In this Champions' Network call, do not try to sell, hustle, or take advantage of people. I repeat, *do not try to tell/sell them.* People can smell it and can become quite protective of themselves. I've found that even friends will quickly move into the mode of, *Oh no, my friend/acquaintance is in a new network-marketing scheme and they want to recruit me. How do I get off this call?* While you shouldn't make any effort to sell at all, with this strategy you *are* selling simply by having a nice conversation. (You'll find the suggested scripts for this call later in this document.)

9. Establish that this is just a "stay in touch" call. Tell them

that life is too short not to stay in touch with the people you've met. Ask them about their business, their family, their hobbies, and what's happening in their life and business.

10. Then take a few minutes to tell them what you're now doing for a living. Let them hear your passion for what you do. Don't be afraid to get a little excited about what you do and what you're doing.

   a. Keep it friendly and honest. Have some fun. You're just talking to a friend (or a perceived friend). Keep the conversation honest to eliminate the perception of a hidden agenda.

   b. Be excited and be passionate. I use an opening line like this one quite often: "You know, I've made a pact with myself to keep in touch with the people I meet and do business with or try to do business with. The world gets to moving too fast these days, and I wanted to at least try to slow it down a bit by being a better communicator and friend. So here I am. What's happening with you these days?" (The complete script follows.)

11. Again, learn about them with honest interest.

12. Always ask to get their current email, home phone, cell phone, business phone, and email from them in order to update your files. Then give them your information as an update.

13. As a closing item, mention that you would appreciate them remembering you if they ever come across anyone who might need the services you offer and, if they

ever do, to please give you a call. (Many people I've approached in this way have said to me, "You know, I might be interested in what you do myself!") It's amazing how well this works!

14. Follow up with an email at the end of every day of calling, reiterating what you discussed on the phone call. Include all your phone numbers, email information, and web addresses. You might also provide an attachment with some "selling" information like a list of frequently asked questions or a version of Meet the Coach kind of marketing information.

We've started to build your personal referral pyramid. You now could easily have over 200 people consciously or unconsciously thinking about you. Because of your effort, the first person they hear mention that they're looking for someone with your expertise will cause them to go into their mental reference file card system and they'll refer you.

You will be amazed.

SELLING WELL ALWAYS PAYS!

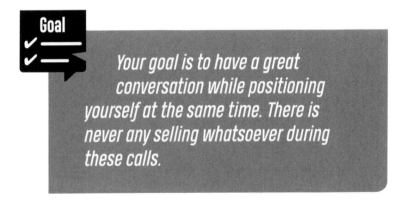

Goal

Your goal is to have a great conversation while positioning yourself at the same time. There is never any selling whatsoever during these calls.

CHAPTER 3

Building Your
SUPER CHAMPIONS' POWER
REFERRAL NETWORK™

PHASE ONE: We now make another list. This second list is one comprised of "influencers." They become your Super-Champions'© list. These are people who could be very strategic for you. These are businesspeople and successful entrepreneurs with connections. They simply know lots of people. They are people who, if they believe in you and what you're doing and see your passion, might be capable of building you an entire practice. This list is usually only about twenty names to begin with and will become eight to fourteen names on an ongoing basis.

1. Start this list by identifying those people and firms that might already target your perfect prospect, or people who

are well-connected. Some of my early Super Champions were successful financial advisors, commercial real estate professionals, Chamber of Commerce executives, successful insurance advisors, CPAs, and local entrepreneurs.

2. Personally call these people. Ask them to meet you for a quick lunch or coffee.

3. Look them in the eye and tell them the same thing you told the others on the phone, but this time you're doing so in person and with passion.

4. Now, let them see and hear your passion about what you do.

5. Here's the key. Inherently, people are nice and want to help. So, ask them for their ADVICE and their HELP. These are two key and strategic psychological trigger words, especially with business leaders with strong "driver" or "analytical" personalities. You are recognizing their importance and success. You're playing to their ego and, when asked, they are always open to offering advice.

   a. Ask them this: "I'm trying to build my business as fast as I can and I'm working hard to do so. But I could use some advice and help. First of all, what business advice, based on your personal success, might you give me about building my business quickly? Listen, listen, listen. Then you'll say something like, "You are an influential person and I would be grateful if you could help me meet anyone you know who might benefit from my service."

   b. An alternative, or maybe an addition, to that

comment is, "Do you know anyone who, by working with me, would make *your* life easier?"

6. That's right, gang. Ask them right then and there if they know of anyone or if they have any customers who might need business coaching services or whatever kind of service you offer. I've found that they will often tell you of someone who comes to mind. They could tell you they've been looking for the kind of service you offer, too.

7. It's funny, but it's my experience you will get one of four answers:

   a. YES

   b. NO

   c. YES, but why didn't you ask me?

   d. NO, but why didn't you ask me?

8. If they have someone they would recommend you speak to, ask them if they would call to give you an introduction. By the way, most will do just that.

9. Be creative. Ask if they might host you for a luncheon or a meeting with their customers. Look for a big niche opportunity. I had a financial planner invite me to speak at his quarterly luncheon for the CPAs he represented. He specialized in CPAs. Eighty-three people attended!

10. Start following the lines and connecting the dots and you may find a honeypot of opportunity right in front of you.

11. Ongoing Application:

   a. Use both of your lists for ongoing and simple

marketing.

b. Use the Champions' Power list and send a weekly or monthly email blast.

c. Use the list for a monthly drip campaign.

d. Use the lists as a feeder to a monthly newsletter mailing.

e. Every business card I ever get goes onto one of these two lists. Everyone you meet is a potential referral agent. It takes some practice to constantly focus on finding and adding potential referral agents but once you get there, your list will grow exponentially. I am constantly adding to my Champions' Power referral list.

f. Again, everyone I meet—and I mean *everyone* I meet in a business or casual setting who would not be a Super or Elite Champion—goes on my Champions' Power Referral list. As I mentioned above, this list is also my newsletter mailing list. So, once a month, they all get my newsletter, thus keeping my name and brand in their mental file-card system. I currently have over 6,000 names on my newsletter list, fully expecting that one of them could give me a lead or become a lead/client if things change in their life.

g. I also jump on the opportunity to "touch" each prospect in numerous ways. I might send out famous quotes I've come across; I might create some sort of special short-term pricing on coaching materials; I might share new customer announcements. The idea is to touch prospects with information that

I'm offering—without any obligation—that might be interesting, helpful, or educational. When this happens, prospects begin to see you in a different way. They begin to see you as someone they might be able to really care about working with and they become sincere and passionate about doing so. In short, things that I feel will appeal to them, so they will see me as someone who "gets" them and their business.

h. Exposure, exposure, exposure. Frequency, frequency, frequency. It's all about maintaining top-of-mind awareness with your potential prospects and customers.

12. Constantly Update Your Super Champions Power Referral Network. Some people will drop off, and you should always be adding others. Meet with them face-to-face at least once per month to share leads, update them on what you're doing, and to constantly ask for referrals or suggestions. Make them feel important to your success. They are! If after a few months they don't produce, drop them from your list and find others to add to the list. ALWAYS be looking for new Super Champions, people who know people you need to know.

Goal

Create your Super Champions list and begin to engage with them.

TWO BONUS STRATEGIES

BONUS ONE:
Getting super-tough doors to open

THE BUSINESS REFERRAL CENTER

Building your Super Champions' Power Network can have other huge advantages. One is in building a fantastic strategy to open doors that would normally be hard to get through. Here's how it works.

In my coaching practice, I am constantly being told by clients that the reason they do not have certain essential services (insurance, legal documents, etc.) is that they don't have time to source and weed out the necessary providers. To facilitate this process and create a valuable resource for clients, I identify and fully vet potential partners to recommend to them. This benefits me in two profound ways:

1. I provide a resource that will save a client's time and energy and create a fabulous tool to help ensure client retention!

2. Through my sourcing and vetting process of finding and filling my Business Referral Center with service professionals that I can now refer to my clients, I have also implemented a very cool and creative strategy to also find and nurture prospects for my own business. In working and referring my BRC people, I'm also directly building a relationship that I hope will turn them into customers for my business. And keep in mind that some of these people might never give me an appointment if

I approached them solely to sell them my product or services.

I created a service within my coaching practice called the Business Referral Center. The service is composed of a list of trusted providers that I can refer to clients and friends who need business services but don't have the time or energy to interview and find the right person. My list consists of about fifty different business services that my clients needed at one time or another. The list includes:

- Business attorneys, patent attorneys, divorce attorneys, etc.

- CPAs and bookkeepers

- Website developers

- Financial planners

- Security providers

- Insurance agents and commercial insurance agents

- Real estate professionals

- Commercial real estate professionals . . . and many others. (A full list and scripts for how to approach them is attached as Addendum #1.)

I target professionals in each of these areas and call or approach them with the request to interview them as someone who would go on my Business Referral Center list of sourced and vetted professionals that I might refer to my clients. Most, if not all, just tell me to put them on my list.

I never do that.

I emphasize that I need to look them in the eye and ask them some questions in order to be comfortable recommending them to my clients. I tell them it is important to be able to say that I have vetted these resources—and it is.

I regularly maintain and add to my Business Referral Center list, and I refer clients to people on this list on a regular basis. There a few rules to this game that you need to know.

1. Never ask for or expect any kind of payment for making this referral. That will ruin the effect of the strategy. The Business Referral Center is totally and completely a service that I offer to my clients and yours should be set up the same way.

2. My goal is to always have at least two names to refer to my client in each of the fifty-plus categories on my list.

3. The list is closely held and protected. I never give out copies of my list and only share the categories.

4. If a client needs a referral to one of the professional services on my BRC list, I always call the source on my list first to see if they are accepting leads. If they are, I then do an introduction of my professional services referral source to my client. This way, the professional referral source knows I am actually working to help them by giving them a quality referral.

5. I always use the professional services' partner vetting meeting as a foundation to also explain what I do and to learn what the professional does.

With the correct line of questioning, a need for my coaching services will emerge. Through this process I have conducted over 500 interviews and I can guarantee you it's a fantastic way to keep your sales funnel full! The goal is always to get in the door, and some of the hardest doors to open will often become your finest clients or resources.

Needless to say, this is a powerful and effective process and a great way to "kill two birds with one stone" by building your Business Referral Center list while, at the same time, get in front of potential prospects.

BONUS TWO:
Be ready for anything!

THE "CURVEBALL" OPPORTUNITY

In my business-coaching practice, I sometimes ask the Super Champions' prospect to tell me what they do to grow their business. Sometimes they surprise me by saying something like, "Well, I appreciate you asking, but not much has been going lately, so I'm not sure I'm the best guy to be talking to!"

So, what do you do? If you're a sharp, active listener and a focused salesperson on a mission, you should be ready for anything. In this case, you should always be ready to move from a referral conversation to a selling conversation. You should be poised to quickly and smoothly transition from the discovery mode of asking questions to focus on working towards gaining a potential client. Be ready and prepared for the "curveball" opportunity, one where your purpose changes on the spot.

When the conversation takes this direction, the Super Champions' Power prospect has just openly, although sometimes not as directly, proclaimed that they are looking for some professional coaching/advisory help and now have officially asked if you could help them. When this happens, this does not mean that the Super Champion cannot still be a Super Champion for you. What it means, however, is that they might also be your newest client. Based upon their personality profile (DISC) some will be more direct than others. (See the addendum for more about DISC.) Some will simply plant hints that all is not right in their business world. So be ready for this curveball. When it is tossed your way, you now have the clear opportunity to say, "Oh really? I'm sorry to hear that. What makes you feel that way?"

Listen, listen, and listen. Then you might say this: "What you just described is exactly what I help business owners like yourself solve every day. Can we take some time and specifically discuss your challenges and opportunities? I want to understand your needs and issues from your point of view. To do this, I would like to ask you some questions so the answers will tell me more about what is going on in your business. More importantly, this will give you an idea of whether it makes sense for us to work together to get you moving forward again. Can we do that now, or would tomorrow at 10:00 be better?"

It's a good idea to take some of your company brochures with you, to have a business card, and maybe have on hand some information about you or what you offer. But always, always, always be ready to do an on-the-spot needs-assessment and be ready to close a new client if the opportunity arises. IF you find this kind of immediate interest and need, DO NOT WAIT to talk with this new prospect. Do not set another meeting to discuss their needs. If they have brought up the need, the need then is a *hot* topic. Never let it cool. You don't need another meeting to establish need. Every prospect, in their own way, is begging you to help them. Some will be direct while others will be more casual, but if they bring it up, it usually took a lot of guts to do so. If they're ready to talk about their issues, then talk about their issues. Don't let them off the hook.

One additional thing that I've found to be powerful is your proper use of words. One word I never use is *problem*. Many business owners with a strong personality profile will immediately throw you out if you suggest they have a problem. This becomes a blatant accusation that they possess a weakness of some sort.

Practice using replacement words. Some examples might be:

REPLACE PROBLEMS WITH CHALLENGES
REPLACE WORRIES WITH ISSUES

The last thing you want to do is to unknowingly embarrass or offend your new prospect by insinuating that they are a poor businessperson. You'll be doomed before you ever get started. You need to become acutely aware of who you are dealing with and what they are asking for.

I was with a salesperson recently who did not heed these premises. When confronted with his "boomerang" opportunity, the first thing he said was, "So, tell me about the problems in your business that keep you awake at night!" To which the prospect said, "Who do you think you are? You've known me for about ten minutes and you're assuming I have problems! That I'm incapable of running my business! Sir, this meeting is now over. You can leave now!"

Look, when selling you have to be ready for anything. A common missed opportunity is when a salesperson is so focused on one opportunity that they miss another. The approach I'm teaching works, and when precisely applied a "boomerang" awareness allows you to consistently acquire a number of quality new clients in your first sixty days. It just a matter of how hard you want to work to build your Champions' Power Referral Network. This is an effective and profitable way to monetize your efforts.

So, get busy!

CHAPTER 4

Building Your Elite Champions' Power Referral Network

THE ELITE CHAMPIONS' POWER REFERRAL NETWORK is situated at the top of the pyramid for a reason. These special partners will become, if managed correctly, powerful Elite partners who consistently remain key to your targeted and focused business-plan map. They are the top of the food chain and different types of Champions, ones who are very distinct from the others.

Each Elite relationship is really about building a partnership. A strong Elite Champion is formed when you work with business owners in a way where there is a benefit for each of you. This will come in the form of a mutual offering of your respective services to each other's clients and contacts. Your Elite Champion is usually not a customer, so your initial approach should never be because you are contacting them as a prospective client.

This is not a sales call.

Your approach from the beginning is one of purely a *strategic partnership* arrangement.

Your Elite Champions are targeted businesses and business owners who are complementary to your business, not competitive. Most importantly, you have the same "perfect customer" profile.

A key factor here is that you have absolute clarity about who your exact, perfect, target customer is. Without this information, you cannot target an Elite Champion correctly.

 **Now we go to work**

With the "Eye of the Entrepreneur" you search for complementary businesses that fit your profile of an Elite Champion. This profile is discussed in length later, but for now the basics are the following. An Elite Champion is one who:

- Has the same target audience as you

- Offers powerful services to your mutual target audience

- Has a strong relationship with their client base

- Is seen as a Trusted Advisor with their client base

- If your Elite partner's customers/clients bought from both of you, the budgets would come from different buckets

Once you find someone who fits your profile, you set a meeting with the purpose of discussing a partnership proposal. Your proposal is one of an invitation to *explore* whether or not a strategic business partnership would make any sense and be beneficial for both parties.

No money is exchanged.

This is merely an opportunity for both parties to offer each other's services to those clients who would benefit from each company's services. This is similar to (but not) a VAR (value-added reseller agreement). This is an unwritten and mutual partnership with the same goal.

The benefits are huge, and the risk is low, with virtually no cost involved. All that I want from the Elite Champions' Power Referral Network partner strategy is eight to twelve Elite Champions who deliver at least two high quality leads to me each year. And just to be clear, when you receive a lead from an Elite Partner, it is not a warm lead. It is as close to a done deal as you will ever get. It is usually pre-sold for you because your Elite Champion's recommendations to his clients are every bit as powerful as yours will be to him or her.

The key benefits of the Elite Partner program are:

1. You create a powerful, effective, and replicable referral/prospecting strategy.

2. You have a group or "team" of highly elite business professionals selling your services for you.

3. When you get a referral, you know it will be a quality referral and usually it will come in at a higher than standard rate.

4. You can manage your time like an Elite professional and efficiently build your business more profitably.

Here are a few examples of great Elite Champions' Power Referral Network members.

As a business coach, my perfect target client is a businessperson/business owner who is doing well and knows they're doing well, but they also know they could do better and that there is another tier of success that they may not know how to achieve.

A great Elite Champion might be an "elite" type of financial planner or advisor, a business broker, or a high-end commercial real estate professional who targets successful businesspeople with a high-end asset base. One of my first Elite Champions was a very successful financial planner. He had the same target audience as mine, and he actively pursues finding his prospects and clients. His issue was that while working with his clients and managing their money and investments, the clients often confided that they had some business issues and asked him for advice—advice which he was often unqualified to answer. By supporting each other, he has a powerful alternative and actually a value-added solution. In the past, he would recommend a consultant, advisor, or coach that he met at a Chamber of Commerce meeting. Many times, they tried to "steal" the client and sabotage his strategies. Now, because of our Elite Champions' Power Referral Network partner agreement, when he's faced with business questions unrelated to his specialty he says, "I hear this often and in response to my customers' needs I have sought out and now offer my customers the services of a world-class business coach in addition to my other services. We will help you solve business issues and grow your business, while at the same time manage your growing money and financial management issues through one coordinated and consolidated strategy."

I CALLED.
I HAVE A NEW CUSTOMER.
WOW!

Talk about a step above a cold call! I've got a lead—a warm lead—a smoking hot opportunity! His recommendation creates the perception that my coaching is part of the services that he offers all his clients. *This sizzling referral comes more like an assignment than a referral.* I don't care if he positions me as a new part of his business, because on this deal we both win. I, in turn, do the same for him with my business coaching clients who confide that they need a quality financial advisor. So, of course, your Elite Champions should definitely be on your Business Referral Center list.

Again, everyone wins.

The value that my Elite Champion partner gets is immeasurable. He gains incredible new marketing opportunities, obtains an increased perceived value of his services, and on and on. There is never an expectation of an override, rewards, or a bonus other than the satisfaction and value in having a powerful "team" of professionals who constantly think about referring me and want to collaborate and complement my business as much as I do theirs.

Another example of a strong Elite Champion partner is the business development executive at any major business bank. I work with one who has a monthly luncheon at a restaurant in the central city area for his new banking customers and prospects. Those invited to this monthly event are all successful businesspeople who have been asked by their elite and trusted banker and bank to attend this luncheon on an "Invitation Only" basis. Only thirty seats are available. As my Elite Champion partner, I am the sole business coach invited to this event. The bank's business development executive introduces me as his go-to business coach. I'm also asked to speak at least once per quarter. I've never left one of these luncheons without at least four appointments with prospective clients.

PREPARE FOR SUCCESS

I always caution people when using this system to be prepared. Believe me, this is not a used-car salesman pitch. Be prepared for the success that WILL happen. At times it will seem as if prospects are falling out of the sky into your lap. Once this system is put into place correctly, and you work it as specified here, the process will run itself.

THIS IS A PERPETUAL-MOTION LEAD-GENERATING MACHINE.

Don't question it, just run with it. Don't be surprised at the ease of attracting and closing customers. Prepare for success.

Goal

Search for 8 to 10 complementary businesses that fit the Elite Champion profile. Set meetings with each to discuss a potential partnership.

CHAPTER 5

An Additional and VERY Important List

WE'VE ESTABLISHED THAT ONE OF THE greatest forms of financial leverage is one's contacts. So far, we've explored three levels of contacts: 1) Champions: People you know; 2) Super Champions: People you know who know people who are key spheres of influence; and 3) Strategic Business Partnerships.

However, there is an additional level of contacts that is just as important (and may become your most important) but this level takes longer to develop. Knowing the "right" people and being known by them can open doors for you that can save you years of hard work. You must develop this advanced level of contacts, so let's make another list.

Make a list of the twenty-five people you feel would be most useful for you to get to know.

It's more than likely that you do not know these people yet! You find these people in the news, on television, in the business journals, in industry newsletters. Who are the key people in your industry or in business that, if you knew them, could help you be successful? Develop a strategy to meet every one of them over the next twelve months.

List the people in charge of major corporations who you might find it useful to know. List the mayor, list the congressmen, and list your senator. Once you've made this list, decide how you could meet them. Now, make a list of twenty-five more!

One more thing . . .

NEVER, EVER FORGET THE REFERRAL POWER OF YOUR EXISTING CUSTOMERS!

Once your business is rolling, never forget your existing customers are a prime resource for new leads and referrals. Every one of your customers should be on your Super Champions' Power Referral Network partner list at the least.

The Harvard School of Business says (and has for years) that at least fifty percent of *new* business each year for every business should come from existing customers.

The secret is that few businesses ever ask their customers for additional business or referrals. I have found that customers are often seriously offended when you don't "honor" them by asking them for referrals. They *know* people who could help you, but in most cases, they don't just offer a list of their friends and business associates. You must earn that right and, again, in most cases you must ask for it.

Research shows that the more affluent the contact is, the

less likely they will be to just give you a referral, so you must ask them for one. They will be protective of their friends and contacts.

They're like anyone else. They want you to earn the privilege of access to their contact lists instead of initiating the act of helping you. So, ask them on a regular basis. Make it a habit! But don't make it hard. If you have a good to great relationship with your clients, then it should be easy at some point to say, "I want to ask you a favor. I'm honored to be working with you and I sincerely appreciate your continued commitment, hard work, and focus. Would you be willing to recommend me to any of your business friends and colleagues so I can work with them at the same level that we have enjoyed?"

There are many ways to ask for a referral but keep it simple and keep it sincere and you will be amazed at the results and the potential goldmine of hot leads directly available for you!

CHAPTER 6

Options and Rules of Professional Networking

STRONGLY BELIEVE THAT THE CHAMPIONS' POWER Referral Network is the most effective and natural, time-efficient way that I have ever discovered for results-focused networking. It is a system that takes into consideration multiple, proven strategies but in a wildly simple system that turns the fear, pressure, and effort of networking into a simple and enjoyable conversation.

Okay, let's pause here. Did you grasp what I just said? This entire process should always be part of a simple and enjoyable conversation. The conversation should always be focused on the goal of discovering together, through discussion, if the two of you should be working together in some way. This approach eliminates the other person's fear of being sold. Hopefully, they understand that the discussion is just a conversation to discover if either of you could be of benefit to the other.

Getting the Discovery Meeting

There are a ton of options for you when it comes to networking. But before we dive into those, I want you to know about some specific steps you can take to maximize your networking efforts.

1. Be sure your target audience is in attendance. I'll describe in detail this issue and how to protect yourself in the next section below, The Networking Trap.

2. If you know your true prospects are at the event, set a results-oriented goal. Attend this event with intent. I never go to a networking event without telling myself how many appointments I will get before I allow myself to totally relax.

3. Understand this: Everyone at the event knows why you're there. You are there for the same reason they are—to make contacts and find potential clients or partners. I'm telling you this, so you (hopefully) are never reluctant to ask someone who fits your profile for a meeting. Ask! The attendees expect it!

4. Shake hands and find out who each person is and what they do. The key element we're looking for is if they are a decision maker for their company. You don't really want to talk with anyone else.

5. There are three elements that you want to satisfy before asking someone for a discovery meeting. We'll review these again later in a different context.

a. Are they an owner or decision maker?

b. Do they understand what you do?

c. Can you identify an immediate need that you might be able to solve for them?

6. If these fall into place, then use this script:

"I'd really like to sit down and talk with you. This place is too loud and impersonal. I would like to ask you just a few questions, the answers to which will help us discover fairly quickly if it makes any sense at all that we should work together. The fact is, I'm not right for everyone. So, can we set a time to just talk this week? Wednesday morning works well for me, or Thursday afternoon if that would be better. Which time works the best for you?"

7. Set the appointment and sync calendars, then . . .

8. Move on to the next prospect. One appointment down.

9. Never allow someone to trick you into asking your questions right then and there! That is simply a veiled objection to get rid of you. If they insist, move on to the next prospect.

10. When you show up for your "conversation" be sure to use the above script again but with some important changes.

"Thank you for this time. That event was great, but it was loud. If you remember, the purpose of our conversation today was for me to just ask you a few questions, the answers to which will help us discover if it makes any sense at all that we should work together in some way. I like to do this because the fact is, what I do isn't right for everyone. So, I like to just sit down and talk to find out if working together in some way makes sense. If it does, great. If not, then I hopefully have a new friend. So, with that said, can we get started?"

Goal

Create effective discovery meetings

The Networking Trap

Before diving in, be sure that you understand that this thing called networking can be as dangerous as quicksand. It drives me crazy when I hear a businessperson brag that they are a master networker. These are generally people who go to five or more networking events a week. They spend valuable hours and time away from their business and family to hand out hundreds of business cards and get hundreds in return. And yet, they have no new customers, no prospects, not even any suspects.

Networking groups and networking events continue to pop up everywhere. Unfortunately, they've become more of a social gathering, a worthless time-sucking activity, instead of an important business strategy. Here's how this usually plays out: You go to an event, collect tons of cards, and then (because you have so many) you procrastinate on your follow-up. You end up with a stack of cards setting on your desk that you don't (or won't) do anything about. They have no value other than to collect dust.

Don't believe me? Okay, try this test. Go to your next

big networking event. Collect all the business cards you can get your hands on. Then, once you get home or back to the office, follow up with every one of the people you received cards from. Once you've done that, then tell me how many people you spoke with who could actually help you move your business or life forward. It's my experience that there won't be many. I call this needle-in-a-haystack networking. You get 100 cards, hoping to find one good one. I don't like those odds.

Here's the rub. At the big networking events, few CEOs, owners, or managers ever attend. They have better things to do. They send staff. These are usually nice people, but few can set appointments, and even fewer have buying power. One of my valued mentors told me something years ago that I think about every day. He said, "Never accept a NO from someone who can't say YES!" This statement became my networking rule of thumb and the key to being more successful in business and spending more time with my family.

Before you attend another networking event, be prepared by first evaluating the event. If it doesn't fit your criteria, stay at home, go to a movie, watch a game, take the family out for dinner—but don't waste your time at worthless networking.

Here are a few questions to ask before every event:

1. Who is my target audience? Be specific.

2. Will my target audience be at this event? Call the organizers and ask. If they give you meeting hype, then take a chance and go one time to find out for yourself. If your target customer isn't there, don't go back to this event ever again. Your specific customer must be in attendance or it's simply not worth your time.

3. If they will be there, what is my specific goal for attending the event? It should not be to collect cards. It should be to set an appointment for a discovery meeting. It should be to set a coffee meeting with someone so you can be introduced to someone they know. Make your attendance productive. Gathering cards is not productive.

4. If your target prospect will not be at this event, figure out where they go to mix and network. Then go there!

It's not about size of the event, it's about the quality of the attendees. Personally, I won't go to a networking event larger than about thirty people and when I do, the event has to be specifically aimed at my target audience.

If networking events are your thing, then do your thing. If you're a professional business-card collector while you're having a cocktail and talking loudly, then get after it. But, for me, if I'm allotting time from my business, family, and life to attend an event, I plan to make it worth my time. I'm looking for people who I can help to achieve their goals and who can help me achieve mine.

I'm going to work.

But enough preaching from my soapbox, let's talk some specifics. There are various networking options open to anyone selling anything today. Here is a list of five options from which to choose. We will start with what I believe is the biggest and most convenient.

Local Chamber of Commerce

Your neighborhood Chamber of Commerce can be a powerful tool for small businesses. Membership will usually include 300+ businesses, even in the smaller Chambers. The opportunities abound to do some solid networking. So, don't let anyone say otherwise. Chambers in your area are huge untouched hotbeds of potential customers for you and your business. In under three years, I pulled in twenty-three new customers from my local Chamber of Commerce and did so at minimal acquisition cost. In fact, the only cost incurred was the price of my Chamber membership and that, my friends, is reason enough to take a long look at this untapped opportunity. It's a prime example of Guerilla Marketing. HIGH value, LOW cost, and a spectacular way to build your Champions' Power Referral Network.

Here is a brief review of the dos and don'ts for establishing your own Chamber strategy.

Basics

1. It does not matter how small your Chamber is. If it's a functioning Chamber, you can make it work big time for you and your business.

2. Visit all the Chambers in your area and find the ones where you (and your strategy) will work best.

3. You're not joining your local chamber to "be an active part of the community and to have a way to pay something back." You're there to find new customers. Period. End. That's all.

4. Almost every Chamber, in every town no matter its size, has a handbook for their regular events. Almost all will have a series of monthly events that will include:

   a. a monthly MORNING mixer.

   b. a monthly EVENING mixer.

   c. a monthly "Meet Your Chamber" breakfast for new members.

   d. one to four or more targeted networking groups that meet on a regular basis.

   e. an "ambassador" group or committee that promotes the Chamber and conducts weekly ribbon-cutting events for members.

   f. a brown bag lunch series with various speakers weekly or bi-weekly.

   g. at least three major events every year (some have monthly events, but most will focus on major events), i.e. Golf Tourney, 4th of July Fireworks Show, Spring Fling, Summer Expo, Christmas Event, etc.

   h. various niche-oriented organizations within the Chamber. For example, Women In Business is usually a strong group.

   i. They will also all have Chamber newsletters and weekly e-mail blasts of some kind including, Member News, Ribbon Cuttings, and a Newsletter.

   j. There are also opportunities to join the Chamber Board of Directors. This should be your target. This is where the real movers and shakers are, and probably where your top prospects are, too.

5. Chambers and their staff are always looking for ways to help or enhance their membership services for their current membership and to attract new members! This opportunity opens up many different ways to offer your product or service as a value-added feature to Chamber membership.

Cautions

1. Try to stay away from the large Chambers. At least give them extra diligence. In these organizations you just don't have a chance to own your niche as much as you would in smaller organizations. Their member events tend to be just big events with lots of "grab and grip" situations. In other words, they're large networking events where everyone has a drink in one hand and a handful of business cards in the other . . . and that's all you do: hand out cards, shake hands, and never have the chance to build relationships.

2. Avoid falling into the Chamber's black hole of committees. Committees are your worst enemy. You'll be required to go to a bunch of organizational meetings and planning meetings and not really get to work your magic on the membership.

3. Your goal is to be the big fish in a small pond, and you can't do that on a committee. Find out what and where you can get the most attention and dominate a space.

Winning Strategies

1. There are three people in every Chamber that you want to make friends with: The Chamber CEO, the Membership Director, and the Marketing/Events Director.

2. Meet the CEO. Ask this person how you can help.

   a. "I want to help you provide some exciting new services to your membership. I'm uniquely qualified as a _____ and I'm here to help you. How can I do that?"

   Look for collaborative ways you can help their membership be better at business. Here are a few ideas:

   a. Offer a complimentary coaching/training session for all new members so they can learn about your product or service.

   b. Include a free product or service certificate in all New Member packets.

   c. Do a monthly business seminar.

   d. Offer a highly discounted rate to any Chamber member if they should want to use your services.

   e. Offer to teach any member how to build or deliver a better "elevator" pitch. (This is a powerful strategy.)

3. Again, remember this: you want to be a BIG FISH and you want to position yourself in a dominate place, so ask them where there are holes in what they want or envision for the Chamber. For instance, my Chamber wanted to have multiple networking groups. I offered to

start one that was business-growth focused instead of just exchanging business cards. I said I would do it if:

    a. they promoted it on a weekly basis in the Chamber Newsletter.

4. I was the ONLY coach or consultant in the group! They said yes, of course. Offer to speak at the New Member Breakfast every month to welcome new members and offer them a free product or services certificate and a discounted rate to the product or service as a new member. Only give the certificate to those who say they will use it and always have your schedule with you to set the complimentary meeting on the spot!

5. Again, the only "committee" that I would ever tell you to push to get on is the Board of Directors. This is a good one, with positive and involved business owners and one that can consistently give you a unique perspective about what's happening.

6. Offer to write a regular article for the Chamber Newsletter.

7. Offer to speak (they're always looking for speakers) at a Chamber event. As a Chamber member, you might get opportunities that usually go to some out-of-town motivational expert. I regularly speak to organizations like Women in Business at their big quarterly meetings. Usually there are over 100 businesswomen attending the event and many, if not most, are business owners.

8. Offer group business advisory sessions or offer to start a group business advisory session specifically for Chamber members.

9. Get to know the Membership Director. They'll let you know who they're trying to get to join, who's new, and who's leaving. You might even offer to work with them to help bring on some new members who might find your services enticing.

10. Get to know the Marketing Director. Advertising costs in Chamber publications and for events are usually minimal, and many Chambers will give you free advertising for the first month or two of your membership.

The list goes on and on. Look at it this way. You can join two or three big networking organizations and spend $1000 bucks or more. For the cost of a Chamber membership, you can usually get access to multiple events, clubs, organizations, and hundreds of business owners. What are you waiting for? Be smart and let this powerful customer-acquisition strategy work for you now! It is one of the ultimate low-cost high-value guerilla marketing tactics and an incredible way to consistently add quality names to your Champions' Power Referral Network.

Large Networking Events

Opinions vary on the effectiveness of large, popular events. Personally, I cringe when I hear someone tell me they went to a super colossus networking event. As I explained at the beginning of this chapter, and is well worth repeating, these events are usually a waste of time for a serious networker. People try to validate their time by assuming that because there were hundreds of people at the event, and that they gave out a hundred cards and, in turn, received a hundred cards, that the event was worth their time. So, determining whether the result of this effort was good or not is through clearly understanding the purpose of going to the event. You must ask yourself if you were going to attend a "social event" with a networking theme that's built around giving out business cards or if you were going to the event with the purpose of getting high-quality business leads that when followed up on would further your business or sales goals. On final review of the newly acquired business cards, it's generally observed that less than five percent of these were the cards of decision makers for a business. So, the question begs, how good are these cards then? You spent an entire evening at a big event, had a couple of drinks and some laughs, and got a few viable business cards to follow up on. Again, I don't get it.

My rule is simple. If I ever go to one of these events and spend the evening away from my family and/or spouse or use some of my hard-earned downtime, then I'm going to the event to work. I go with the specific goal of finding and securing quality meetings with those attendees that, as detailed earlier:

a. Fit my perfect client profile

b. Are decision makers

c. Have an immediate need that I can affect

Once I've secured my goal of setting up meetings then, and only then, will I have a beverage or relax a bit. Honestly, most of the time I leave the event at that point. These mega events can be hard work just in trying to find people who fit my profile. I couldn't care less about anyone who doesn't fit my profile. That's why my focus on what kind of events I go to has changed.

Small, Boutique Networking Events

My choice for attending a networking event—and I might add, the most effective of any of the many types of events—are small, boutique networking events. I mentioned one earlier that was effective for me. A member of my Super Champions' Power Referral Network was the new Business Development Director of a large bank in my state. Once a month, he had a "by invitation only" networking event at a local mid-town restaurant. Only thirty invitations went out for each monthly event. The event would be limited to the banker's current commercial customers and his commercial business prospects plus a few other lucky invitees. The luncheon included a nice lunch; a fifteen-minute presentation, which usually focused on local business issues, plus quality networking for the attendees. It was never a sales pitch for the bank.

As a rule of thumb, when attending the mega-events usually less than five percent of those attendees proved to be my prospects. In addition, I also had to find these prospects among the masses, truly the proverbial needle in the haystack.

With small, focused events, ninety-five percent of all attendees are potential prospects and I don't have to spend hours finding them. In addition, everyone at these types of events is there with the expectation that they'll meet everyone, and they fully expect to develop some new and profitable business relationships. In fact, the bank's business development manager's event I mentioned earlier is where I initially found 100% of my Elite Champions and many, many Super Champions. The big differentiator was that this event was presented and endorsed by a trusted advisor (the bank).

Take the time to find events and contacts like these and add them to your networking repertoire. They exist in every market I've ever been in—it just takes some work to find them. They will prove to be an invaluable addition to building your entire Champions' Power Referral Network Pyramid.

Networking Clubs

Many people find that networking clubs can be an effective tool. I also believe they can be an effective strategy, but they are not right for everyone. A few of the most noteworthy ones include BNI (Business Network International), LeTip International, AmSpirit Business Connections, and many, many more. Some are national or even international organizations. There are hundreds of local versions. Just Google www.meetup.com to find a list of all the groups in your market.

Most of these groups will charge a monthly or annual fee to be in the group if accepted. Most will have an acceptance policy based on business category exclusivity. Usually, they have one person representing that person's business niche per group chapter. That would mean one insurance person, one attorney, one carpet cleaning business, one pest control business, and so on. A member may be required to provide a certain number of leads to another member of the group on a weekly or monthly basis. If you are a consumer-based business that depends on a consistent flow of leads and new customers, then these organizations can be quite effective. However, you see the same people at every meeting, and you tell your business story to the same people every meeting. After a while, there is always the chance that these groups will run out of lead opportunities for you. Nonetheless, there is an element of kinship that can develop within these groups. Most have weekly luncheons where every member can feel they're immersed in a safe haven filled with friends with positive attitudes. Many people will be a member of more than one of these organizations.

The biggest issue to look out for, as always, is leadership dynamics. If the leader does not adhere to the "one member per business category" stipulation, this creates a problem. Believe me, it gets uncomfortable if you are suddenly looking at your biggest competitor who has become the newest member of the group.

These organizations can be great ways to add, specifically, to your Champions and Super Champions' Power Referral Networks.

Specific Business Category Events

This category would include:

- specific groups such as those for attorneys, physicians, dentists, etc.

- trade organizations

Let's start with specific business groups. If your product or service is targeted at a certain type of group, then it would make sense to focus on that group. Almost every city and state has groups and associations that have regular meetings attended by and for specific groups such as attorneys; physicians in general, and specific practice categories like cardiologists or oncologists; dentists; chiropractors; and many other professional groups. Two things are always a constant. One, they almost always have a membership category for vendors or comparable associate memberships. And, two, they are always looking for guest speakers who are also associate members. This can be an incredible way to become known to your specific prospect base.

The other side of this category is trade organizations. Again, most cities and states have trade organizations whose memberships are comprised of many kinds of businesses that all typically deal with a certain industry. For instance, I've worked with the Petroleum Marketers Association or APMA. Members of this trade association include any marketer of petroleum products, including wholesalers and retailers, vendors, suppliers, and other supporters of the industry. This could include anyone from construction companies who build convenience stores, to the trucking company that delivers fuel, or the technology company that sells and services fuel pumps. Simply speaking, if you are targeting any element of this industry it would be worth buying, at minimum, an associate membership and then attend the meetings so you can meet multiple prospects in one place at least once a month.

There are trade associations for most industries from real estate to petroleum and all categories of medicine, healthcare, communication, technology, and more. Again, based on your target audience, this could be a target-rich environment in which you can build a high-quality Champions' Referral Network Pyramid.

No matter the options you choose, the Champions' Power Referral Network process is, or should be, your goal. Everything you do should have an eye toward enhancing your Champions, your Super Champions, or your Elite Champions' team. Do not waste your time on any activity that does not contribute to the growth and empowerment of your Champions' Power Referral Network and building your army of referral agents!

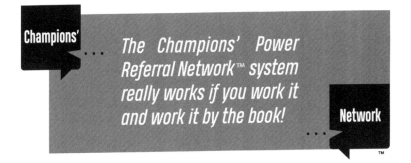

The Champions' Power Referral Network™ system really works if you work it and work it by the book!

CHAPTER 7

Final Thoughts

O NE OF MY MOST CHERISHED MENTORS once told me that the major similarity between a forty-story skyscraper and a three-bedroom house was that without a solid foundation both would fall over. The same analogy applies to building a strong business. The foundation must be based on proven principles applied with dedication and conviction. The Champions' Power Referral Network provides that proven foundation and backbone that will help every business owner achieve their goals faster and with greater success.

Here are a few "written in stone" foundational rules of successful networking:

RULES OF PROFESSIONAL NETWORKING AND REFERRING

1. **NEVER EAT ALONE!** Breakfast or lunch is a great time to build a network and personal relationship with a targeted Super Champion or Elite Champion.

2. PEOPLE LIKE TO **REFER** PEOPLE THEY KNOW, or think they know, and trust.

3. PEOPLE LIKE TO **HIRE** PEOPLE THEY KNOW, or think they know, and trust.

4. PEOPLE LIKE TO **RECOMMEND** PEOPLE THEY KNOW, or think they know, and trust.

5. PEOPLE LIKE TO **BUY** FROM PEOPLE THEY KNOW, or think they know, and trust

Okay, it's time to get busy and get to work. Prospects and customers will fall from the sky at your feet . . . but you must work the system. It sounds a bit crazy I know, and some of you who have made it this far in this book are probably now saying, yeah, yeah, yeah. Here comes the hype.

Believe me, it's no hype.

I am living proof of the effectiveness of this system, just as thousands of others who have implemented this process will attest. This is a logical and quickly implementable system. It systematizes many of the options that you might already use and adds new elements and strategies that together make it a powerful, world-class tool. The fact is, the Champion-building process changes how you think about prospecting, priority management, and selling. Ageless research repeatedly proves that if you positively change the quality of your thinking that over time amazing things begin to happen. If you move from a survivor mentality to a to one of a thriving mentality, this shift in your daily attitude will clarify your purpose and clear the path for untold success.

But you must be willing to change and adapt. You must eliminate any activity that steals precious time from your day by focusing on low value, low consequence activities. You must redirect your personal power to high-value, high-consequence activities that result in powerful levels of success.

That is the power of the Champions' Power Referral Network.

There's an old saying that came from the cattle drives of the old west. The adage applies to business today more than ever and is a key factor in how you could look at life and your personal success.

If you were on a cattle drive and lucky enough to be at the front of the herd with the lead animals, the air was always fresh, the wind was in your face, the horizon clear with lots of potential. If you were in the back of the herd, the sights, air quality, and scope of your view was limited. The old cowboys would say (and the adage focuses on the only two options you really have in life):

You're either makin' dust or you're eatin' dust!

I prefer to be "Makin' Dust!"

I prefer to work hard but work smart and efficiently.

I prefer to be willing to change and adjust . . . and

I prefer to WIN!

The only thing left for us is to get to work and apply these principles:

- **WORK HARD.** Go out and have some fun having great conversations. Talk to people, talk to lots of people, and ask lots of people for appointments. Then don't be afraid to ask them to buy. If you've done your job up to this point, asking them to buy is a logical next step and part of the process.

- **WORK SMART.** Always work smart with a laser-sharp focus on looking only for those potential prospects who fit your Perfect Prospect Profile.

- **BE A PRIORITY MANAGEMENT FREAK.** Only concern yourself with high-value, high-consequence activities and never waste a moment on random activities with low-consequence results, particularly when it comes to your prospecting activity. The German philosopher, Goethe, said, "Never allow the most important things in life to be at the mercy of the least important things." And he said that in the late 1700s, so it's not a new concept.

- **WORK YOUR NETWORK.** Diligently create and

consistently master your own Champions' Power Referral Network. It is the foundation and nerve center for all your sales and, for that matter, marketing activities.

- **HAVE A CLEAR CALL TO ACTION.** Never force a prospect to guess what you want from them. Always have a clear "call to action." Always know exactly what you want your prospect to do next and don't be afraid to ask them for it.

- **CLEARLY ASK FOR A BUSINESS COMMITMENT.** Many people who sell a product or service are afraid to close the deal. Again, closing should be a logical and incidental act. Look, let me let you in on a little secret. Your prospect or client knows why your there. You are there to do some business, so don't act like you don't know or understand that. It's a waste of your time and a waste of your prospect's time. Do not say, "So what do you think?" Be clear of your intentions and say, "Based on what we've discussed here today, can we begin working together on Monday?" Easy peasy. What's the worst that could happen?

And finally,

- **ALWAYS BELIEVE IN YOURSELF.** If you don't believe in yourself, believe you're the best solution for any prospect's needs on the planet Earth, the prospect will smell your fear and lack of confidence and they will run away. And if they don't run away, they will at least say *no*! When no one else believes in you, you must believe in yourself with all your heart and soul. You've got to walk, talk, smile, and stand like you are the number-one authority on whatever it is that you're selling. If you don't believe it, your prospect won't either.

That's not too much to ask in return for the potential reward, is it?

> Good luck, and as always,
> make every day count!
>
> Coach Dan

Business Coach Dan says
Together, anything is possible!

Give me a call at (602) 697-5949 to see how you or your team can increase your business by working with me! There's no obligation but it may be the best thing you've ever done for yourself and your business.

CHAPTER 8

Champions' Power Referral Network™ Telephone Scripts for Recruiting Champions and Super Champions

Champions' Power Referral Network™ Calling Script:

HERE ARE SOME TELEMARKETING AND FOLLOW-UP email scripts to use when you implement the Champions' strategy:

1. Initially, the people you call for your first-level Champions' list are all friends, people you know, think you know, or they think they know you and/or your reputation. Keep

in mind that you are not making a single traditional "cold call." This is a call to someone who is familiar, and it is a "conversation" call, not a sales call. If you sound like you're going to sell them something, you'll lose them.

2. Be conversational and remember to *sell by not selling!* Brian Tracy says that *The Law of Inadvertent Selling* applies here. This law says that by not openly selling, you are selling by implanting an idea into the person you have called. The idea behind this call is multi-purposed.

   a. Say hello and re-connect.

   b. Just chat for a few minutes

   c. Ask about them, then update them on what you're doing!

   d. Don't ask them directly about coaching but ask indirectly. Ask for them to be sure to recommend you as a referral to a friend or acquaintance who might be a candidate for coaching.

   e. Keep the conversation loose and friendly and don't spend a lot of time.

   f. Again, if you try to sell, think you're smart and try to slip in a sales pitch, you will be dead in the water.

Champions' List Telephone Script:

*Hey, _____ (your name) **here. How are you?***

How's the family? (If appropriate)

Say, the reason I'm calling is just to reconnect a bit. I've

made a new commitment to myself to not let life get to moving so fast that I lose contact with friends. That seems to happen easily these days. So, I made a list and I'm calling everyone just to take a minute and catch up.

So, what are you doing these days? (Probe and ask a few questions that show your interest. Let your contact talk as long as they want, and you will eventually get around to a point where they will ask you what's up in your life!)

Well, I've still got several irons in the fire. You know me. But there's one thing I am doing that I'm really excited about. I am a _____ now and I feel like I was born to do this work. I really enjoy it.

I work with small businesspeople, entrepreneurs, and sole proprietors to help them achieve their personal and business goals much faster than they normally would. The work is gratifying. There's a proven system that I use that was, in part, developed by Brian Tracy, one of the top business-development experts in the world. Along with that, I incorporate my business experience and that's what makes the results powerful.

Anyway, I'll get a plug in here and ask that if you ever come across anyone who could benefit from business coaching, please pass my name on to them.

Hey, _____ (their name), *it's sure been great to talk with you. Say hi to the family for me. Do you have an email address? If you don't mind, can we exchange contact information and such? Thanks, good to talk again. See you!*

Email Follow-Up Message

NOTE: Now, as soon as you're done with every batch of calls, every day, immediately send a form email out that says something like this:

> *"Greetings _____. Just wanted to thank you again for taking some time out of your day to chat (today/yesterday). As I promised, here is all of my current information. (Email/cell #/ home phone/work phone/website address).*
>
> *Let's not let the speed of life get in the way of connecting. And remember if you come across anyone who might benefit from business coaching, be sure to let me know!*
>
> *Thanks again. Let's keep in touch!"*

You might want to attach an informational document about you and/or something about your business, benefits, etc. It's just an obvious opportunity to do some free, low-cost/no-cost marketing.

It's rare that I ever need to call anyone on this list again. At this point, they all go onto my newsletter mailing list and will be "touched" every month by my newsletter. By the way, when I initially did this, I had a 100% opt-in rate to my newsletter invitation! Incidentally, it's the law that you ask people if they want to be on your email list, you can't automatically add them, so be sure to do this the right way.

The result of this work is that you now have POSITIONED yourself in the minds of 200+ or so people who will unconsciously think about you, then once someone in their circle mentions their need for coaching, they will consciously remember you and, hopefully, refer you.

This is the first big step to building your referral army and sales force!

SUPER Champions' Power Referral Network™ Telephone Script

Level two in building your Champions' Power Referral Network is to build your Super Champions' Network. The Super Champions' Power Network strategy is quite different than the Champions' Power Network script. The idea here is to be talking with the handful of influential people who you might have initially found on your Champions' list. These are people who know lots of people that you need to know. Some of these people will come to you immediately. Some will come to you as you build your initial Champions' List.

To begin with, let's define the word *influential*. In this application, the word represents who you might know that, as part of their business, just knows a lot of people who could be either your customers or people that you need to know. One of my first productive Super Champions' Power Network members was a major real estate broker in my area. He knew everyone I needed to know and gave me one of my biggest prospecting days ever! One lead this Super Champion gave me turned into eighty-two qualified leads, fifty presentations, fifteen proposals, and twelve new clients.

Another influential Super Champions' Power Network partner was a successful commercial insurance professional. He insured thousands of business owners in the region. By the way, he later became one of my customers and continues to be a client eleven years later.

Your goal with this call is to set a coffee or lunch meeting so you can get face to face and share your passion for your business and then ask for their advice and help (by giving you a referral) to kick-start your business and grow it as fast as possible.

This script is much more direct in purpose. There are two powerful and distinctive strategic versions of the Super Champions' Power Network script that you might use.

TELEPHONE SCRIPT: VERSION #1

Hi _____ (name), *this is* _____ (your name). *It's good to talk with you.*

I'm calling to ask you for some advice and help. I've always heard great things about you and your business knowledge. I'm trying to build my business as fast as I can and I'm working hard to do so. But I could really use some advice and help on how to build my business faster. Can we meet sometime soon for some coffee or a quick lunch so I could ask you a couple of questions and get some advice on how you have been successful?

(NOTE: Keep in mind the BOOMERANG opportunity that might come up here. Be ready for anything.)

THE BUSINESS REFERRAL CENTER/SUPER-CHAMPION HYBRID SCRIPT

"Hi _____ . *Thanks for taking my call. I'm calling to ask you for some advice and help. I'm* _____ (your name here) *and many of my customers are always looking for professional services. So, I would like to talk to you about joining my Partner*

Referral list that I use and offer to all my customers because I would like you to be on that list. That way, if a customer needs a _____ *then they don't have to go look for one since I've already done the research and can send them to people on my list. I'd like to talk briefly about that.*

The second thing I would like to do is to ask you a few questions to get some advice on how I might continue to build my business. It's that simple . . . and I'm even buying. (Laugh) So how does your schedule look for coffee on Wednesday morning, or would Friday at noon work better?"

Do NOT get off the phone without an appointment unless your Super-Champions' prospect is absolutely a dud and just doesn't want to take the time. In that case, thank them and move on and find another Super Champion! The key words here are ADVICE and HELP. I've seldom been turned down by even a "driver" personality when I have properly asked for their advice.

When you go to the meeting, have fun and keep it very loose. But be passionate about what you say and about what you do. Make it clear how much you enjoy helping people with their success. If the Super Champions' Power Network prospect sees your passion, they not only will be glad to give you a referral but will often want to know more about your work themselves.

Script for the In-Person Meeting

"Thank you for your time today. As I mentioned on the phone, I'm trying to build my business as fast as I can

and I'm working very hard to do so. But I could use some of your advice and help. First of all, what business advice might you give me about building my business more quickly? What are some of the things you have done to grow faster than average?

Listen, listen, and listen. Then:

Wow, thanks for that input. I really appreciate your thoughts and learning from your experience. I've taken notes and if it's okay may I call you if I have any questions?

Thanks again, and as I mentioned, along with the advice I also need your help. I know that you know lots of businesspeople and I would be grateful if you could help me meet anyone you know who might benefit from using my product/service. Is there anyone you can think of right now?"

Don't be surprised if they do more than give you some names. I have often had the Super Champion offer to contact the lead and set up the meeting for me or at least offer an introduction.

Remember, you will only receive four possible answers:

YES, I know someone

NO, I don't know anyone right now

YES, I know someone I can recommend now, and I might be interested as well

NO, I don't know anyone right now, but I might be interested!

The Business Referral Center Scripts

In today's challenging economy, a businessperson cannot afford the time and money involved in searching, finding, and analyzing every critical business relationship. The Business Referral Center (BRC) was created to provide you with the strategic business relationships you need, all available in one location. BRC has pre-screened and interviewed professionals in key business assistance categories essential for surviving and thriving in today's business climate. Every member of the BRC community is a known, trusted, and proven expert in their field. They are professionals you can rely on to assist with your business growth issues.

- **Save time.** All BRC members are accessible through one resource: Business Coach Dan Creed. No more tiresome hours of research and interviews.

- **Save money.** There's no fee for the service and you save immediately instead of making a costly mistake and then needing to find a different resource.

- **Save frustration.** Eliminate the worry of finding the

right strategic partner. Source who you need, now, by calling the Business Referral Center.

Advertising services	Flash Design
Accounting	Franchise Broker
Banking	Franchise Brokering
Bookkeeping Services	Health Insurance
Branding Services	Internet Marketing
Business Banking	IT Management
Business Brokering	Legal: Business Law
Business Coaching	Security
Business Decorating	Legal: Immigration Law
Business Exposition	Merchant Services
Capital Funding	Mortgage Lending
Chiropractic	Outsourced Accounting
Comm. Construction	Payroll Services
Comm. Real Estate	Photography, Business
Commercial Insurance	Printing Services
Computer Repair	Project Management
CPA Services	Public Relations
Dentistry	Publishing
Digital Media Services	Sales and Marketing
Employee Staffing	SEO
Equipment Leasing	Social Media
Executive Development	Web Design
Financial Planning	

Business Referral Center™ Scripts: Telephone or In-Person

You: "Hi Mr. Contract Lawyer. My name is
_____ and I'm a Business Coach
here in _____. I'm calling because I
need your help. I work with business owners to
help them grow their businesses and improve their
lives. I work with both small and large businesses
every day. One of the most frustrating things I hear
every day is when my clients have a need for a key
business service but don't know who to contact.
Often, they don't have access to these business
services because they don't have the time to do the
research, do interviews, and hold meetings to find
the right fit for things ranging from legal services
to commercial insurance. It got so frustrating for
me that I'm doing something about it.

"I've created a free service for my clients called
the Business Referral Center (BRC). I believe there
are over fifty B2B services that clients are looking
for. I've taken on the task of finding one to two
providers in each category, then I interview them
and place them as a member of the BRC. In this
case, I need a contract lawyer. Would you have
some time to meet so I can find out about your
practice and you can learn about what I'm doing?
If it's then appropriate, I can hopefully add you to
the BRC Referral List."

Lawyer: "Oh that sounds great! You can go ahead and

include me!"

You: "I wish I could, but I've promised my clients that if I give them a Business Referral Center referral that I've vetted the recommendation and that I personally stand behind their credibility. So, I actually need to meet with you. When would be a good time? I have some time open on Wednesday around 10:00. Would that work for you?"

Lawyer: "Okay, Wednesday will work. So, if I'm approved, when can I get a list of the other businesses in the Business Referral Center?"

You: "Here's how it works. The list is confidential. I never reveal who's on the list. I'm in control of it always. When I have a client who needs a referral, I tell them I have two business professionals that fit their needs. I then call you and see if you are willing to meet with them. If so, I will either give you their names or I will give them your name so they can contact you. Whichever is best for you. Okay? See you Wednesday. I can give you more details then."

DISC/Psychometric Profiling and Its Application for Networking

History

I REMEMBER THE FIRST TIME I WAS INTRODUCED to the DISC assessment. It was 1979 and as part of our sales training regimen I was asked to take an assessment. Friends, this was in the Stone Age. We didn't have cell phones or computers. We did the assessment truly old-school using only pencil and paper. I still have my first DISC assessment.

I was blown away at how exact it was. It pegged me precisely when it came to my personality traits, why I did what I did, and what my motivation was for doing it. Since then, the science of Psychometric Metric Profiling has dramatically evolved. So, let's take a moment and look at its history and exactly what it has to do with prospecting for clients and networking.

The concept of Psychometric Profiling has been around a very, very long time. We've found references to it as far back as 400 BC where Greek physician, Hippocrates, refers to his theory of The Four Temperaments. Fast forward a thousand years or so and the idea of understanding people based upon their personality DNA is still around and is still getting attention.

In 1928, psychologist William Moulton Marston bursts onto the profiling scene. Marston was already known as the man who created and administered the first polygraph test. With his groundbreaking research, he advanced the science of psychometric profiling with his book, *Emotions of Normal People*, where he identifies four distinct personality traits: dominance, influencing, steadiness, and conscientiousness. The book is one of the first to clinically explore people's sense of who they are and their interaction with their environment.

In 1956, industrial psychologist, Walter Clark built what is considered the first behavioral assessment tool that served to confirm Marston's theory of the DISC model. In 1965, Peter Merenda and Walter Clark published their findings on this new assessment tool. The findings were published in the *Journal of Clinical Psychology*. Then, less than ten years later, John Geier created *The Personal Profile System*.

Psychometric Profiling was originally designed to be a powerful tool for recruiting. Today it is used for myriad purposes including recruiting, leadership training, counseling, and selling. The science has been advanced to incredible levels and, in turn, many companies have created their version of the assessments but all, to a degree, use the same science. Companies offer systems such as the Myers-Briggs Type Indicator, the Keirsey Temperament Sorter, the Hermann Brain Dominance Instrument and, of course, different companies represent DISC, the godfather of them all.

Application

For purposes of this short tutorial, I will use the acronym from the original research, DISC. The power in DISC is to make you a communication superstar. Understand your prospect's profile and you understand how to approach them, how to talk with them, and most importantly, how to sell them on anything. The four profiles are:

D — Dominance

I — Influencer

S — Steadiness

C — Conscientiousness

Rather than get into a full discussion about Psychometric Profiling and DISC, I want to focus this addendum on how DISC can incredibly improve your odds when it comes to networking, prospecting, selling, and retaining new clients. My next book will show you how to master the power of psychometric profiling with simple to learn processes than are both immediately applicable and practical. Until then, here are a few key things to remember.

1. Remember these three words: Adapt, Manage, and Influence. When you learn to identify the personality profile of your prospect or client you can then deal with them based on their specific personality profile.

2. Once you respond to their specific profile, you become

someone who, in their mind, really understands them.

3. If they feel you understand them, they will feel that they can trust you and can tell you things.

4. When they tell you things and you shut up and listen, they will buy from you.

5. Once they buy from you, you can then manage the relationship in adherence to their personality profile and they will want to work with you longer, thus creating a powerful client retention tool.

6. If you retain the client for a long time, you become their trusted advisor and can influence them to do positive things for their self and for their business.

Understanding the Profiles

Here are a few identifiers for each DISC profile and how you might adapt your approach for each personality in order to sell to them.

D: DOMINATOR

Traits: All business, non-emotional, gets right to the point, wants clarity, has a no-nonsense approach, very direct.

Adapting: Gets to the point quickly and stays away from small talk. Establish why you're there and what you want. When they're ready to buy, let them buy and don't talk yourself out of a sale.

I: INFLUENCER

Traits: Enthusiastic, passionate, inspiring, seeks

recognition, warm and talkative, positive ego, trusting.

Adapting: Exchange energy with this person but don't let them get off on tangents. You can easily talk for an hour about the weather or the big game just to run out of time and find that you never spoke about business.

S: STEADY

Traits: Very risk-averse, wants relationships, is emotional, trusting, anxious and fearful, wants guarantees, references, and assurances.

Adapting: The key word here is RISK AVERSE. Tell them you understand that they might be concerned about risk and then show them how you will eliminate any of their perceived risks with your deal.

C: CONSCIENTIOUSNESS

Traits: Wants proof, lacks trust, non-emotional, cautious, needs things in writing, naturally suspicious, wants evidence.

Adapting: The C needs proof and time to analyze, so if you're trying to set an appointment with them be specific about your purpose and the amount of time necessary for the conversation and details. Use lots of logic with proof to back it up. They like anything that includes testimonials, case studies.

There is so much to discuss about this subject but start by becoming more focused on observing and listening. When you do, you can both see and hear people's personality traits emerge. Then, and only then, can you adapt to people and influence them simply by relating to them.

For full information on booking Dan Creed
for personal or professional business coaching,
or to speak at your next meeting,
please visit www.realworldbusinesscoach.com
or call us directly at (602) 697-5949

BONUS!

For even more business guidance
from Coach Dan, here's an excerpt from

The No Baloney, Bottom Line on Success!

The hardest part about achieving success is the discipline required. The foundational elements of success are straightforward and simple. It's the day-to-day commitment and discipline to make these basic elements a ritual that's tough. In fact, most people can't do it. That's why you see so few people who are exceptionally successful. The true secret to the exceptionally successful individual is usually

Straight Talk....... *The true secret to the exceptionally successful individual is usually their soul-deep commitment to the basics and the massive action necessary. Translation: they are committed to their vision, and they work hard.*

their soul-deep commitment to the basics and the massive action necessary. Translation: they are committed to their vision, and they work hard.

Here are what I believe are the foundational commitments and mindsets necessary for success. Keep in mind these apply without regard to location, your age, income, or education, no matter your background, and in any economy. This is where it all starts. If you are not a master of these commitments and this mindset, no fancy strategy or fads will work.

1. **Attitude** — Go ahead and laugh. Everybody says attitude is key. The question I have is this: how many people practice having a good attitude? The Carnegie Institute says that of all the traits observed in successful people, eighty-five percent of their success is attributed to *attitude*. By the way, skills and knowledge only represent fifteen percent of the total attributes needed to achieve success.

2. **Decisiveness** — You must decide to be successful. If you're happy with where you're at right now, so be it. But if you honestly have a burning desire for the next level, commit to it or please, just shut up.

3. **Hard work** — If you want to be successful, if you want to be an entrepreneur, then know that eighty-five percent of success happens with sixty hours of work a week or more. You work forty hours a week just to get a paycheck and for survival—anything over that is what sets you up for success.

4. **Self-discipline** — Zig Zeigler once said, "If you're hard on yourself, LIFE will be easy on you." You must have the willingness to do whatever it might take to succeed (with integrity, I must add). You must be a master of self-discipline, defined long ago as, "Doing what you need to do when you need to do it, whether you want to do it or not."

5. **Set priorities** — If you start your day performing and completing a major task, the research shows you perform the rest of the day at a higher level. In turn, if you

start your day with emails and trivial matters, then it is also proven that you work at a much lower level the remainder of the day. So, make the adjustment now. Start every day with your highest-priority task. Ask yourself, "What is the consequence if I do this task or not?" If the consequences are high, do this task first. If it's a low-consequence task, simply don't do it.

6. **Single-mindedness** — It takes a minimum of five times longer to finish a job if you start, stop, start, and stop. You must put your head down and focus and get it done, eliminating any unnecessary interruptions.

7. **Open-mindedness** — You must be willing to take everything you know and potentially unlearn it, then relearn new ways of doing things. The fact is, in today's rapidly changing world, if you don't have an open mind and you continue to do business the way you've always done business, then you undoubtedly will be out of business.

8. **Risk-taking** — Sometimes you simply need to take a calculated risk. You can't be afraid. Your best opportunities may be lost simply because you took too long to think about them.

9. **Taking responsibility** — No more complaining, no more blame, no more excuses, and no more problems. A situation is only a problem if you don't learn something from it. Take charge of your life, take responsibility, and figure out a solution, learn, and move on.

10. **Be willing to change** — You must be willing and able to change, adapt, and adjust at a moment's notice. The

market and consumers will not wait for you. The ability to adapt and change is imperative if you want to be an entrepreneur.

11. **Gaining total clarity** — You must constantly learn, grow, and ask questions in order to discover those elements that will affect your life and your business. Things are changing at a pace never before seen. You must examine everything, then examine it all over again. You must challenge everything, then do it again. You must question everything, again and again. Always be testing the market, reading reports, and doing market research to gain more and more clarity on your business and all that might affect it.

12. **Have written goals** — A business or person without goals—written goals—will never reach their potential. Here are the facts: seventy percent of our society don't have *any* goals. Twenty-eight percent say they have goals, but they are not written down. Two percent of the population (or less) have written goals. But here is the kicker. The two percent with written goals control more revenue than the other ninety-eight percent combined. Is that incentive enough to have clear, concise written goals?

13. **Learn to sell** — This is a requirement, a necessity with no exceptions. No matter what you think about people who sell, you had better become proficient at it. You must sell if you want to be an entrepreneur and own a business. So, read some books, take a class or seminar, hire a sales coach—do whatever you have to do, but learn to sell. It is imperative in life.

14. Be happy — Simply, you must love what you are doing. If you don't, it shows. So, do yourself a favor, heck, do me a favor and just get out of business. Get out of the way of others who are passionate about what they are doing and then go find something you are, or can be, passionate about. Life is too short not to enjoy what you're doing.

Now is the time to hone your skills; it is not the time to coast. Remember, you can only coast in one direction. Never coast—you can't afford to.

Planning for Success: Purpose

I recently heard a comedian say that this year was so bad "I ordered a burger at a fast food place and the kid behind the counter asked, "Can you *afford* fries with that?"

How was this year for you and your business? That's the question every business owner is asking, or should be asking, themselves at this time of year. Unfortunately, a high percentage of business owners are afraid of the answer, many times because they don't *know* the answer, so it's easier to avoid the question.

Now is the time to face the facts. Did you have a good year? Did you have a bad year? What did you do right? What did you do wrong? What can you do better?

Now is the time to ask the questions, face the answers, and begin to plan. The time to begin planning is not annually in January; it is now.

One of my favorite quotes comes from John Richardson, American author and academic. Mr. Richardson said in 1938, "When it comes to the future, there are three kinds of people: those who let it happen, those who make it happen, and those who wonder what happened."

Which one are you?

There are an estimated two million business start-ups annually. It is estimated that nearly ninety percent will fail in two years or less. Eighty-six percent of all businesses are operating below their potential in sales and profitability. The fact is, most entrepreneurs have not really started a business but have instead created a job for themselves. A job where they are working harder, for longer hours and for less pay.

Consultants know that there are many reasons that a business might fail and most of the reasons have nothing to do with the economy, who's President, or market issues. The most common of these reasons are:

1. Lack of direction and goals

2. Impatience—they want too much too soon

3. Greed

4. Poor cost control

5. Poor quality of product

6. Insufficient capital

7. Insufficient sales

Altogether, this list simply says that businesspeople who struggle have seriously underestimated the amount of time, effort, and money required to be successful. Almost all these points come back to a significant lack of planning. So, it's time to plan, beginning now . . . beginning today. To do this, you need clarity. Without clarity, you are only working in the shadows and using best guesses—and that never works. Make a commitment to set a new path, a new discipline to raise yourself and your business to a higher plain. Otherwise, you may end next year wondering what happened . . . again.

P is for Success

Every year I try to force myself to do a ceremonial CLEANING OF THE FILES. I go through (or at least try to) every file in every file cabinet in my two offices and recycle or throw out unnecessary paper, folders, notes, and sundry materials. It could be said that I am a hoarder of sorts with business materials. I know it sounds goofy, but I have attended or been a part of some remarkable sales, marketing, and business training in my career so far. The materials and notes from these meetings are incredibly valuable when you look at them from the perspective of their collective effect on my career. their collective effect on my career. Heck, I still have notes from sales meetings I attended in the 1970s. You never know when that information might come in handy, right?

While deep into this year's attempted purge, I came across a tattered, torn, yellowed 5"x7" file card. The writing on the card had almost faded but was still legible. Held together with tape of some kind, I could still make out the note which was important enough for me at one time to put this one concept on the card. It was titled "The 6 Ps of Personal Success."

Some people today might scoff at this kind of motivational mantra but to me and others who truly commit themselves to long-term personal growth and development, the message here is timeless. So, with that, let me share with you something from my archives.

The 6 Ps of Personal Success

1. **Purpose** — I have dedicated the time and effort to create

and maintain well thought out, written goals. I have taken the same care and diligence to focus on analyzing and clearly understanding my values. These two things will shape my future and everything I do. These goals will be the guiding light for all my future achievements.

2. **Pride** — I get up every morning with the ability to say, "I feel good about myself." I understand that I don't need the acceptance of other people to feel important. I love what I'm doing, and I am passionate about it.

3. **Patience** — I believe that things will eventually work out well. Particularly if I believe they will. I don't need everything to happen instantly.

4. **Persistence** — I stick to my purpose, especially when it seems inconvenient. I live in the immortal words of Sir Winston Churchill, "Never, Never, Never, Give Up."

5. **Perspective** — I take time to enter each day quietly, in a mood of reflection, to get focused and listen to my inner self to see things more clearly.

6. **Passion** — I am passionate about what I do every day. Passion attracts people and opportunities. Not crazy, wild-eyed passion, but passion that shows in all my actions, in everything that I do and say. The day I am not passionate about what I do, I will re-focus and find something else I can be passionate about.

I hope that this serves as a reminder that it's the simple, basic, and foundational things that will get us to where we're going faster than the latest fad.

"Don't make a major business move until you read *Straight Talk . . . Thriving in Business*. This book will walk you and your business through the basics and put you on the right track to boldly move forward. Roll up your sleeves and do a few warmup exercises before sitting down with *Straight Talk . . . Thriving in Business*. And, don't miss the 40% Rule on page 75."

MARC MCCOY
AUTHOR of
The Time of My Life Began When the Doctor Numbered My Days

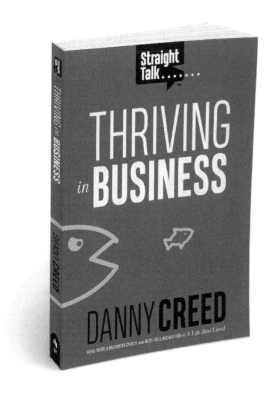

Danny Creed's book,
Straight Talk—Thriving In Business,
is available wherever books are sold.

> "Forget about all the other books about business success. This is the only one you need. The recipe is here, all you need to add is the effort."

MICHAEL R. MARTENS, MANAGING PARTNER
FIRST STAFF BENEFITS LLC

the publishing CIRCLE

ABOUT THE AUTHOR

Danny Creed ...

MASTER BUSINESS COACH Danny Creed is an award-winning international master business and executive coach, business consultant, trainer, entrepreneur, best-selling author, and world-class keynote and workshop speaker. (www.realworldbusinesscoach.com). He is a recognized expert in sales, management, and start-up business strategic planning. He is also a business turnaround and marketing specialist with a strong emphasis on business development and business growth strategies. Dan is an elite Brian Tracy International Certified Sales Trainer and a Founding Member

Trainer and Facilitator of the Brian Tracy Global Corporate Training Courses and the Sales Success Intensive course. Coach Dan has logged nearly 15,000 business coaching, consulting, and training hours and counting. He has been involved with fourteen successful start-up businesses and over 400 business turnaround challenges. Coach Dan is the unprecedented SIX-time recipient of the FocalPoint International Brian Tracy Award of Sales Excellence.

In December 2011, Coach Dan released his first book, *Bootstrap Business*. The book was a collaborative effort as part of an established and highly successful book series with world-renowned business development experts, Tom Hopkins (*How to Master the Art of Selling*), John Christensen (*FISH!*) and Jack Canfield (*Chicken Soup for the Soul*). His best-selling second book, *A Life Best Lived; A Story of Life, Death and Second Chances* is available worldwide on Amazon.com and Audible, or www.businesscoachdan.com/author.

He is also widely published in numerous magazines around the world including *Business Coach Magazine*, serving Eastern Europe and *Business Venezuela*, the official magazine of the Venezuelan-American Chamber of Commerce.

• • •

To contact Dan for executive one-on-one coaching, workshops, or keynote speaking:

Phone: 602-697-5949
Email: Danny@MrLuckyCoaching.com
Web: www.realworldbusinesscoach.com
LinkedIn: www.linkedin.com/in/businesscoachdan
Newsletter: https://www.fpinl.biz/16/newsletter

• • •

OTHER BOOKS BY DANNY CREED

Straight Talk on Thriving in Business

A Life Best Lived

COMING SOON:

Straight Talk on Marketing—
$50,000 Work of Free Marketing

Straight Talk for Becoming
a Communication Superstar

Straight Talk on Setting and Achieving
Your Goals

Straight Talk—Sales Communication Blueprint

Straight Talk on Mastering the Grind

• • •

For full information on booking Dan Creed
for personal or professional business coaching,
or to speak at your next meeting,
please visit www.realworldbusinesscoach.com
or call us directly at (602) 697-5949